What It Means to Be a Christian

Written by
Andrea Brock Denton

100 Devotions for Girls

978-1-4336-8569-9

Published by B&H Publishing Group
Nashville, Tennessee

Dewey Decimal Classification: 242.62
Subject Heading: SALVATION \ DEVOTIONAL LITERATURE \ GIRLS

All Scripture quotations are taken from
the Holman Christian Standard Bible®, Copyright ©
1999, 2000, 2002, 2003, 2009 by Holman Bible Publishers.

1 2 3 4 5 6 · 18 17 16 15

Contents

Introduction

Why is this book in your hands? Are you wondering what being a Christian is all about? Do you feel God pulling on your heart, telling you He wants you as one of His own?

It's time to put your faith in Jesus and make the decision that you will never regret. Let these Scriptures and devotions help you work through your questions and show you that a life lived through Christ offers you grace and forgiveness, purpose and peace, and an undeserved eternity with Him in heaven. *That* is what it means to be a Christian.

Rescued

**For I am not ashamed of the gospel,
because it is God's power for salvation to everyone
who believes, first to the Jew, and also to the Greek.**

—ROMANS 1:16

Every human being who has lived, is living, or will live is born a sinner. Our sin separates us from the perfect and holy God, and it requires a payment of cleansing blood to reconcile us to God. The gospel is God's rescue plan for sinners. Christ's death and resurrection are the power to save those who believe. Christians celebrate their rescue. There is no shame or embarrassment in being rescued.

In the Old Testament, God chose to rescue a group of people called the Israelites. In the New Testament, God engrafts non-Israelites into His chosen people. "The Jew" (an Israelite) and "the Greek" (anyone who is not an Israelite) are both rescued by God through the sacrifice of Christ. This is the ultimate rescue, and it is available to the person who opens her heart to God's rescue by trusting in Christ's death and resurrection.

What do you think it would feel like to be rescued?

I think it would feel so wonderful and awesome to be rescued that I can't even explain it!!!!!

A few years later... I am 13 and I now think that being rescued would feel like amazing because then you would notice, "oh, someone really does care about me! WOW" and I would feel very loved.

God's Heavenly Kingdom

**The Lord will rescue me from every evil work
and will bring me safely into His heavenly kingdom.
To Him be the glory forever and ever! Amen.**

—2 TIMOTHY 4:18

When God rescues you, you have the promise of being with Him in eternity. God's heavenly kingdom offers endless perfection, goodness, and love. Imagine your best days and your favorite memories. You do not want those days or memories to end. This is how you will feel in eternity with God. You will never want the goodness, joy, fun, and laughter to end.

The only qualification for being with God forever is to place your trust in Christ and live by faith. A life lived with Christ as your Lord, Savior, and King ends, or really begins, with being ushered into His heavenly kingdom.

Imagine heaven. What will it look like? How will you spend your time?

I think even will be beutiful and have a lot of prietty flowers on the edge of the golden path leadlng to the golde kingdom. I will probably spend my thim talking to God (Asking him a lot of qwestions), Jesus, people and took around.

Made Blameless

For all have sinned and fall short of the glory of God. They are justified freely by His grace through the redemption that is in Christ Jesus.

—ROMANS 3:23–24

Imagine that you took a test called "God's glory." Making 100 on the test would mean you attained God's glory, but on this test, no matter how many times you took it, you would never score a perfect 100. You would always fall short of achieving that 100, and not because you did not study or did not pay attention in class, but because you had a condition that kept you from making a perfect score. Now imagine that someone took the test for you, under your name, and made 100, and that 100 was credited to you! That is what Christ has done for you.

Every person falls short of the glory of God because we have all sinned. Sin is what separates us from God, yet God sees us as blameless, as making the perfect score of 100, because Christ's test score stands in the place of our imperfect score.

Where in your life do you try to be perfect?

_____

_____

_____

_____

_____

_____

_____

_____

_____

_____

_____

_____

_____

_____

_____

Recognizing Our Sin Nature

Therefore, just as sin entered the world
through one man, and death through sin, in this
way death spread to all men, because all sinned.

—ROMANS 5:12

When I was pregnant with my boys, everything that I ate passed on to them. This is why pregnant women have to watch what they consume. They are eating for two (or more if they are carrying multiples), so they should not digest anything that would be bad for their baby. The mouth of an expectant mother is the gateway to all the nutrients that flow to her baby. In a similar way, Adam, the first person God created, was the gateway that brought sin into the world. That sin now flows to every single person who has existed or will exist. The reality of the sinful state of humanity may not seem fair, but it is real. We are all sinners.

What are the things in your life, heart, and mind that separate you from God?

_____

_____

_____

_____

_____

_____

_____

_____

_____

_____

_____

_____

_____

_____

_____

5

What We Deserve

For the wages of sin is death.

—ROMANS 6:23

In the Old Testament, God entered into relationships with Adam, Noah, Abraham, Moses, and the Israelites. These relationships were like a marriage, in that God and His people were bound to each other by an agreement they made. This marriage, however, was unbreakable because God never stopped loving His people, and He always kept His word. The other thing different about this marriage was that death was the consequence of the people breaking the agreement. The people would mess up and not show their love for God by disobeying Him, but each time, God remained faithful to His promises.

We, too, are disobedient and mess up all the time. We are sinners just like Adam. Because we are sinners, we deserve death. The death we deserve is being separated from God forever. But this is not the end of the story.

What relationships do you feel bound to?

_____

_____

_____

_____

_____

_____

_____

_____

_____

_____

_____

_____

_____

_____

A Gift We Do Not Deserve

. . . but the gift of God is eternal life in Christ Jesus our Lord.

—ROMANS 6:23

Sin is gross. It is so gross that the holy and perfect God of the Bible cannot even look upon it. Our sin earns us separation from God forever. This separation is the ultimate death because it is where God's anger is poured out on those who reject Him. But God took the punishment of death for us. He died on the cross to pay the penalty of death. His death gives life to those who believe in him. Christ's death gives the gift of life rather than the rightful consequence of living apart from Him. If we accept Christ, we are given an eternal life where we will never be separated from God again. In Christ, we are given the gift of life, which we do not deserve.

Other than God, who in your life treats you even better than you deserve?

_____

_____

_____

_____

_____

_____

_____

_____

_____

_____

_____

_____

_____

_____

7

Christ Died for Us!

But God proves His own love for us in that while we were still sinners, Christ died for us!

—ROMANS 5:8

We think a lot of ourselves, which is partly why social media are so popular. We love to update others about ourselves. We post where we have been, whom we have been with, and even what we have eaten. There is one significant event in life that has nothing to do with our accomplishments and status—salvation. We did nothing to save ourselves. That act of love was all Christ. He saved us, not because of our profile, but because we were in need of being rescued from the death that follows sin.

What is your biggest accomplishment?

Two Gateways

**For just as through one man's disobedience
the many were made sinners, so also through the
one man's obedience the many will be made righteous.**

—ROMANS 5:19

In the same way that Adam is the gateway for sin in the world, Christ is the gateway for righteousness. From Adam flows sin and disobedience, but from Christ flows righteousness and obedience. The difference between these two gateways is that we naturally receive the disobedience from Adam (we are born as sinners), but we have to believe in Christ to receive His righteousness. Christ's righteousness does not naturally flow to us. But when we accept Christ as Lord and Savior, His righteousness covers us, triumphs over our sin nature, and becomes our new identity. We still sin, but we are no longer slaves to sin.

If you had a new identity, which sins would you want to leave behind with your old self?

_____

_____

_____

_____

_____

_____

_____

_____

_____

_____

_____

_____

_____

_____

_____

The Full Gospel

**Since by the one man's trespass,
death reigned through that one man,
how much more will those who receive
the overflow of grace and the gift of righteousness
reign in life through the one man, Jesus Christ.**

—ROMANS 5:17

Being a Christian means that you believe in the death and resurrection of Christ. You believe that Christ lived a perfect life, died a death that you deserve, and conquered death through His resurrection. But the gospel is more than just believing in Christ's death and resurrection. The gospel is also living a changed life because Christ's righteousness reigns in your life now. Christians not only have their sin nature but the righteousness of Christ; therefore, Christians should live out of Christ's righteousness rather than out of their sin.

What is the biggest influence in your life right now? Culture? Family? Friends? God?

_____

_____

_____

_____

_____

_____

_____

_____

_____

_____

_____

_____

_____

_____

_____

Who Influences You?

My son, if sinners entice you, don't be persuaded.

—PROVERBS 1:10

We know from Scripture that every human being is a sinner. There are times, though, in Scripture where *sinners* refers to anyone who is not a follower of God. Proverbs 1:10 says not to let these people influence us. Christians should resist the temptation to talk or act like people who do not know the Lord. Being a Christian means resisting the things that this world tells us are important.

If a stranger watched everything you did today, would she think you followed God or not?

11

Repent

From then on Jesus began to preach, "Repent, because the kingdom of heaven has come near!"

—MATTHEW 4:17

Being a Christian means living a life of repentance. We mess up all the time and need to be forgiven. Our thoughts and the motives of the heart usually have only our self in mind. We are selfish to the core of our being and must turn to Christ to ask for forgiveness. Repenting makes us conscious of our behavior and our need for a Savior. Faith in the blood that Christ spilled for us on the cross is what cleanses us of our sin. We repent not only to be cleansed but also because the kingdom of heaven is near! Christ will return, and our hope in His return is what puts our selfishness in check and prompts our hearts to repent.

How is repentance different than just being sorry?

_____

_____

_____

_____

_____

_____

_____

_____

_____

_____

_____

_____

_____

_____

Life by the Word

He humbled you by letting you go hungry; then He gave you
manna to eat, which you and your fathers had not known,
so that you might learn that man does not live on bread alone
but on every word that comes from the mouth of the LORD.

—DEUTERONOMY 8:3

In the Old Testament, the Israelites were God's people. They were slaves in Egypt, and they cried out to the Lord about their slavery, and God heard them and used a man named Moses to lead them out of Egypt. Moses led them through a body of water that God split in half so that the Israelites could escape Egypt and head to the land God promised them. On the other side, they became thirsty and hungry. Before God gave them water to drink and food to eat, He let them feel hungry so that they would know life comes from the very Word of God and not what they eat.

God gave His Word to the Israelites through His promises and then the Law of Moses. God still gives us His Word today in the books of the Bible. In order to experience true living, we must feed off of His Word.

What is your favorite Scripture and why?

_____

_____

_____

_____

_____

_____

_____

_____

_____

_____

_____

_____

_____

_____

Collections

"Don't collect for yourselves treasures on earth, where moth and rust destroy and where thieves break in and steal. But collect for yourselves treasures in heaven, where neither moth nor rust destroys, and where thieves don't break in and steal. For where your treasure is, there your heart will be also."

—MATTHEW 6:19–21

We all have items we like either to collect or hold onto. Sometimes these items end up on display, in a scrapbook, or in an attic. God tells us not to treasure these material possessions. It is fine to have them, but it is not fine to depend on them for our happiness. God instructs us not to depend on material possessions we collect on earth because they can leave us as quickly as they were given to us. God tells us, instead, to focus on and treasure our eternal home in heaven because it is everlasting. If we lost part of a collection that meant a lot to us, we would be disappointed, and if we lost part of a collection that we treasured, we would be devastated. When our attention in life is on heaven, our hearts will never be disappointed or devastated.

What do you collect? Can you think of nonmaterial treasures to collect too?

_____

_____

_____

_____

_____

_____

_____

_____

_____

_____

_____

_____

_____

_____

"Come to Me"

"Come to Me, all of you who are weary and burdened, and I will give you rest. All of you, take up My yoke and learn from Me, because I am gentle and humble in heart, and you will find rest for yourselves."

—MATTHEW 11:28–29

When I was a little girl, I used to love sitting in my grandfather's lap while he read God's Word. Many times he would invite me to sit with him as he read the Bible. He was a very patient and gentle man, and I felt loved when I was with him. My grandfather is a large part of my decision to accept Christ as my personal Lord and Savior. My grandfather taught me what it looks like to seek Jesus. He taught me what it means to come to Jesus and find rest. He showed me that even though Christ no longer lives on this earth, we experience Him and know Him through the Bible. He demonstrated that coming to Jesus is reading God's Word.

Who first taught you about God? What did you learn?

Don't Listen to the World

Do not be conformed to this age, but be transformed by the renewing of your mind, so that you may discern what is the good, pleasing, and perfect will of God.

—ROMANS 12:2

The age we live in tells girls to be a certain size, attain a certain look, and hold the attention of guys. Scripture, on the other hand, tells us to transform ourselves, not in our appearance, but by repairing our minds. Usually something that needs repairing is first broken. Our minds need repairing because the world breaks them with its lies. Once we restore our minds by turning to Truth in God's Word, we understand what God wants. Being a Christian means to let God, and not the world, be the standard for your thoughts.

Can you think of some specific lies the world is telling you?

_____

_____

_____

_____

_____

_____

_____

_____

_____

_____

_____

_____

_____

_____

_____

Love Others

The commandments: Do not commit adultery; do not murder; do not steal; do not covet; and whatever other commandment— all are summed up by this: Love your neighbor as yourself.

—ROMANS 13:9

Moses, the man God used to lead His people (the Israelites) out of Egypt, was given the Ten Commandments from God to give to the Israelites. The first four commandments have to do with our relationship with God. The last six commandments have to do with our relationship with other people: We are to honor our mother and father, not murder, not commit adultery, not steal, not lie, and not covet. Romans 13:9 says these six commandments can be summed up in one sentence: Love others as you love yourself.

We are all pretty good at taking care of ourselves. When we are hungry, we eat. When we want something, we get it ourselves or ask our parents to get it for us. We sleep when we want and practice what we want to become great at. So when God says to love others like we love ourselves, we are to take care of their needs and wants like we would take care of our own.

Who in your life could use some more love from you?

_____

_____

_____

_____

_____

_____

_____

_____

_____

_____

_____

_____

_____

_____

How Majestic Is Your Name

When I observe Your heavens, the work of Your fingers, the moon and the stars, which You set in place, what is man that You remember him, the son of man that You look after him? You made him little less than God and crowned him with glory and honor.

—PSALM 8:3–5

My husband and I love visiting family in Montana. The beauty of the state overwhelms your sight and stirs your emotions. City lights do not interfere with the stars God has set in place, landscapes go on for miles, and peace is as prevalent as the wildlife. Montana is just one place, in all of creation, to observe the majesty of the Author of creation. Genesis 1 and 2, Psalm 8, and other places in Scripture tell us that all of creation is the work of God.

Mankind is part of the creation of God. Along with oceans filled with aquatic life, the highest mountains, the seasons, and all the galaxies, God created male and female. You are the grandest part of what God created. Your parents knew that when they first held you. God knows it, too, and He loves you with a love that compares with nothing else you will ever experience in this world.

What is your favorite part of God's creation?

_____

_____

_____

_____

_____

_____

_____

_____

_____

_____

_____

_____

_____

_____

The Great Counselor

I will praise the LORD who counsels me—
even at night my conscience instructs me.

—PSALM 16:7

Counselors are patient, good listeners, merciful, and strong. They are gentle with the truth; good at not telling you the answers, but letting you figure them out for yourself; and sympathetic concerning your past or present situation while directing you towards a future of hope. I know this about counselors because I am married to one. I do not know the specifics of what my husband hears in a session with one of his clients, but I do know that his clients come into his office and talk. He might have to draw the talking out of them, but his clients do speak. When it comes to a relationship with the Lord, we are prone to expect Him to fix things in our lives without ever speaking to Him. We must talk to the Lord about our circumstances. God already knows our circumstances, so the talking is for our benefit not His.

Write a prayer to God below as if you were writing a note to your best friend.

_____

_____

_____

_____

_____

_____

_____

_____

_____

_____

_____

_____

_____

_____

_____

_____

_____

Love

Love is patient, love is kind. Love does not envy, is not boastful, is not conceited, does not act improperly, is not selfish, is not provoked, and does not keep a record of wrongs. Love finds no joy in unrighteousness but rejoices in the truth. [Love] bears all things, believes all things, hopes all things, endures all things.

—1 CORINTHIANS 13:4–7

When I was around your age, I heard a talk by a youth minister, and he challenged his audience to read this passage substituting the word "love" with their names. Try it. Look at the verses above, and put your name in place of the word "love." What parts make you cringe when you read it with your name? It is okay when your name turns the verse into an untrue statement because only one name can make this passage read true, and that is the name "Jesus." Only Jesus' name is interchangeable with the word "love." This does not excuse us from showing love, though. Christians are called to love and then to trust Christ's perfectly obedient life and death to cover them when they act unloving.

Is there a part of 1 Corinthians 13:4–7 that best describes the way you love others?

_____

_____

_____

_____

_____

_____

_____

_____

_____

_____

_____

_____

_____

Patient

Love is patient, love is kind.

—1 CORINTHIANS 13:4

I considered myself a patient person until I had children. When my children were young, I wrote this verse on my bathroom mirror with a marker to remind myself to be patient and kind to them. I had to keep this verse before me because the behavior of my two little boys would set me off, and I would react with anger instead of patience and kindness. I hated my behavior. I wanted to get to the core of my impatience, so I prayed a lot about it. God showed me that others' dependence on me triggered my impatience, and He wanted to change that about me. There was no better way to break me of that then to make me a mom!

Look at the situations that bring impatience and unkindness out in you. Ask God to show you why you respond with unkindness rather than love. He wants to change you to make you look more like His Son, who is Love.

Try to sit patiently for the next three minutes without doing anything. What was the hardest part?

_____

_____

_____

_____

_____

_____

_____

_____

_____

_____

_____

_____

_____

_____

The Danger of Comparison

Love does not envy, is not boastful, is not conceited.

—1 CORINTHIANS 13:4

Girls are queens of comparison. Beginning in late elementary school and continuing throughout middle school, a female's focus is on other girls. She watches other girls without saying a word and computes who has what and who excels at what. She inwardly investigates the social and physical development of other girls, the material possessions of other girls, and the academic, social, and athletic abilities of other girls. Then, she decides how she feels about herself based on her research. She either becomes envious of what someone else has or conceited from what she has in comparison to everyone else.

Love, however, does not compare. Love does not envy another person for what she has because love is being content with how God made you. Love is being grateful for what God has given you. Love is being secure in yourself and how God has made you, so you, therefore, have no need to be jealous, boastful, or conceited.

List five unique and wonderful things about the
way God made you.

_____

_____

_____

_____

_____

_____

_____

_____

_____

_____

_____

_____

Rude

[Love] does not act improperly, is not selfish, is not provoked.

—1 CORINTHIANS 13:5

Sometimes we are the rudest to those we love the most. How backwards is that? If we love someone, our words and actions should convey that to them. In what relationships do you act rudely or improperly? Which relationships bring out selfishness in you rather than selflessness? Which of your relationships annoy you?

God calls us to lay down the emotional weapons of rudeness, selfishness, and agitation. Ask yourself if you need to change your attitude towards some of your friendships or some of your relationships with family members.

Would you rather spend time with your rudest friend or your kindest friend?

_____

_____

_____

_____

_____

_____

_____

_____

_____

_____

_____

_____

_____

_____

A Record of Wrongs

. . . and [love] does not keep a record of wrongs.

—1 CORINTHIANS 13:5

When a girlfriend offends us for the first time, we usually let it slide. When she offends us a second time, it is easy to file that offense away with the intention of using it against her later. The more we get hurt by her and never say anything about it, the longer her file of wrongs becomes. If we never destroy the mental file we are keeping of her wrongs, we can easily retaliate one day.

God tells us to destroy the records we keep against people because love cannot penetrate a heart hardened towards others from the internal filing system we keep of their record of wrongs. Instead of focusing on the wrongs of others, we need to take an honest look at our own actions and focus on ourselves.

Are you holding a grudge against anyone? Is it heavy?

_____

_____

_____

_____

_____

_____

_____

_____

_____

_____

_____

_____

_____

_____

_____

_____

Rejoice in the Truth

Love finds no joy in unrighteousness but rejoices in the truth.

—1 CORINTHIANS 13:6

Imagine you have a friend who talks about being a singer, but you know she can not really carry a tune. In almost every conversation, she mentions her vocal lessons and coach. Then one day, she decides to try out for the school musical. That evening you contemplate calling your friend to find out about her audition. You know it could not have gone well, but you want to hear her say it. Then you stop yourself, check your motive, and remind yourself that love finds no joy in unrighteous thinking. You realize that living in the truth—of sin not being your master—is more important than taking joy in your instincts being confirmed that your friend had a disastrous audition.

What are some ways you can be more supportive of your friends?

_____

_____

_____

_____

_____

_____

_____

_____

_____

_____

_____

_____

_____

_____

_____

_____

Believe the Best

[Love] bears all things, believes all things.

—1 CORINTHIANS 13:7

When you have a friend share something with you in confidence, like one of her insecurities, and you keep it to yourself, that is love. You are choosing to bear her burden rather than exploit her insecurity. When your parents say they love you and that they are grounding you for coming home late, and you accept the punishment because you know you were in the wrong, that is love. You are choosing to believe the best about your parents' love for you, even as they discipline you, rather than assume that they are just taking out their frustration on you.

Love bears the burdens of friends, and love believes the best about your parents.

Who in your life has helped bear your burdens?

_____

_____

_____

_____

_____

_____

_____

_____

_____

_____

_____

_____

_____

_____

26

Endure

[Love] hopes all things, endures all things.

—1 CORINTHIANS 13:7

This verse stands out among all the verses about love when you consider your age. There is a lot to endure as a girl who is in the "in-between" years. You are no longer a kid, but you are not a teenager. You have to believe in the things that you cannot see—like that you will grow into your body, and you have to endure all the things that others put you through—like the way you are treated or the comments about how you look.

God calls a Christian at your age to hope for what He can see about your life even though it is unclear to you and to endure all the ridicule you might be facing because He is using it to shape you.

What do you hope for the most?

_____

_____

_____

_____

_____

_____

_____

_____

_____

_____

_____

_____

_____

_____

The Resurrection

And if Christ has not been raised, then our proclamation is without foundation, and so is your faith. . . . But now Christ has been raised from the dead.

—1 CORINTHIANS 15:14, 20

Christianity is founded on the death and resurrection of Jesus Christ. When we celebrate Easter, we are proclaiming the resurrection of Christ that occurred three days after His death. If Christ did not defeat death and rise from the grave, then the Christian faith would have no foundation, and there would be no need to celebrate Easter. But we know, in fact, from God's Word that Christ was raised from the dead.

Sin and death came into this world through Adam and Eve. Ever since the fall of man, every human being has been born into death because of sin. The good news of the gospel, and the foundation to the Christian faith, is that anyone who accepts Christ's death and resurrection is given life through Christ.

Do you think it was easier for those in Bible times
to believe in the resurrection than it is for us?

_____

_____

_____

_____

_____

_____

_____

_____

_____

_____

_____

_____

_____

_____

Out with the Old

Therefore, if anyone is in Christ, he is a new creation; old things have passed away, and look, new things have come.

—2 CORINTHIANS 5:17

I love clearing items out of my house that no longer get used. I keep a permanent bin in the garage for Goodwill. My children are constantly growing, so their gently used clothes and toys go into our yellow bin to make room for their new clothes and new toys. Women's fashion is constantly changing, so clothes that I have not worn after two years end up in the bin to make room in my closet for new clothes. Household items, from what I find crammed in a hall closet to what does not get used in the kitchen, end up out of the house to make room for newer gifts or purchases. This type of "spring cleaning" is exactly what Scripture says to do when in a relationship with the Lord. Except, instead of cleaning out our closets, we clean up our hearts. Our old way of behaving, talking, and thinking must go to make room for the perfect and holy God who resides in our hearts.

Pretend you're spring cleaning your heart, mind, and activities. What needs to be thrown out?

_____

_____

_____

_____

_____

_____

_____

_____

_____

_____

_____

_____

_____

_____

Everything Is God's

The earth and everything in it, the world and its inhabitants, belong to the Lord; for He laid its foundation on the seas and established it on the rivers.

—PSALM 24:1–2

God created every single human being who has existed or will exist. Somehow, we all bear a resemblance to God. We were made in His image whether we act like it or not. We all belong to Him whether we believe it or not. We are his because He is the one who designed us. God also created the world. He had the idea for trees, mountains, oceans, rivers, canyons, blue skies, weather, seasons, sunsets, vegetation, and animals. The world is spectacular, and its inhabitants are the summit of all that He created. We are to treat both with upmost respect. We should not deface either earth or humanity.

How can you better take care of the world and people around you?

_____

_____

_____

_____

_____

_____

_____

_____

_____

_____

_____

_____

_____

_____

_____

_____

Live by Faith

**And I no longer live, but Christ lives in me.
The life I now live in the body, I live by faith in the
Son of God, who loved me and gave Himself for me.**

—GALATIANS 2:20

Most people want instant gratification. We have a hard time waiting on food to be delivered, prayers to be answered, traffic lights to change, technology to work, and messages to be returned. Even drive-through lines move too slowly for us. We want to see results immediately. Living by faith means being okay with not seeing the things we hope for, trusting that those things will happen, and learning to be patient in the meantime.

When are you most impatient?

One Team

For as many of you as have been baptized into Christ have put on Christ like a garment. There is no Jew or Greek, slave or free, male or female; for you are all one in Christ Jesus.

—GALATIANS 3:27–28

On a sports team, all the players wear the same uniform. In a game, there is no confusion as to who is playing for which team. When you accept Christ, you put on His team jersey. When others look at your life, there should be no confusion as to the One for whom you are living.

Outside of wearing the same jersey, your Christian teammates will not look like you. Each player will have a different background, a different story, different looks, and different gifts, but you will all wear the same garment, which makes you one.

What are some benefits of being part of a team?

_____

_____

_____

_____

_____

_____

_____

_____

_____

_____

_____

_____

_____

32

An Inheritance

And because you are sons, God has sent the Spirit of His Son into our hearts, crying, "*Abba*, Father!" So you are no longer a slave but a son, and if a son, then an heir through God.

—GALATIANS 4:6–7

When you become a Christian, your status changes. Your status is no longer "slave," but "child of the King of kings." You bear a title of "Daughter," which means you have an inheritance. Think of what kind of inheritance you will receive from the Author of everything! Your heavenly Father will shower you with all that belongs to Him. Your inheritance is greater than money, and you get to keep all that your Father gives you for all of eternity.

How is being the daughter of the heavenly King better than being the daughter of an earthly king?

_____

_____

_____

_____

_____

_____

_____

_____

_____

_____

_____

_____

_____

_____

Two Natures Battle

I say then, walk by the Spirit and you will not carry out the desire of the flesh. For the flesh desires what is against the Spirit, and the Spirit desires what is against the flesh; these are opposed to each other, so that you don't do what you want.

—GALATIANS 5:16–17

A Christian has two natures. The sin nature she was born into desires sin, and the redeemed part desires to walk in the Spirit. The key to a Christian's freedom comes from her understanding that she is not enslaved to sin. The desires of her flesh do not rule her; Christ does. Christ reigns victorious in her through the Holy Spirit. Even though she will still have times when she does what she knows she should not, her redeemed nature fights against her sin nature. As she grows and matures in her faith, she chooses more and more to walk by the Spirit. She still sins, but she becomes more aware that her flesh is the loser in this battle.

What do you think God wants you to desire?

_____

_____

_____

_____

_____

_____

_____

_____

_____

_____

_____

_____

_____

_____

_____

34

Who Inherits the Kingdom of God?

Now the works of the flesh are obvious: sexual immorality, moral impurity, promiscuity, idolatry, sorcery, hatreds, strife, jealousy, outbursts of anger, selfish ambitions, dissensions, factions, envy, drunkenness, carousing, and anything similar. . . . Those who practice such things will not inherit the kingdom of God.

—GALATIANS 5:19–21

We are inclined to skim over this list of fleshly desires and declare ourselves innocent of all that is listed, thereby assuming we are worthy of inheriting the kingdom of God, but the point of this passage is to show us that we are incapable of steering clear of the desires of the flesh that are listed. Our moral compass may lead us to believe that we are safe from the consequence of moral impurity, but what about the rest of the descriptions listed? Can we say that we have never been jealous, angry, or selfish?

The only person who has never given in to any desire of the flesh is Christ. Belief and trust in Him are the keys to inheriting the kingdom of God.

Jealousy, anger, selfishness—do you struggle with one more than the other?

_____

_____

_____

_____

_____

_____

_____

_____

_____

_____

_____

_____

_____

_____

_____

_____

The Fruit of the Spirit

But the fruit of the Spirit is love, joy, peace, patience, kindness, goodness, faith, gentleness, self-control. Against such things there is no law.

—GALATIANS 5:22–23

If every human being loved, promoted peace, and exercised self-control, there would be no need for laws. We would need neither a justice system nor people who enforce laws if everyone bore the fruit of the Spirit.

The fruit of the Spirit is the standard of living for a Christian and should flow out of a Christian's life. Anyone who accepts Christ is given the gift of the Holy Spirit. God's Spirit, then, produces His fruit in a believer. This production process lasts a lifetime!

Pick one fruit of the Spirit that you think God wants to grow in your life. Why did you pick that fruit?

_____

_____

_____

_____

_____

_____

_____

_____

_____

_____

_____

_____

_____

_____

36

Seek God

I have asked one thing from the Lord; it is what I desire: to dwell in the house of the Lord all the days of my life, gazing on the beauty of the Lord and seeking Him in His temple.

—PSALM 27:4

Think of all the things that you want. When you make a birthday or Christmas list, what is on it? On the psalmist's list was just one thing: to dwell with the Lord every day of his life. The author of this psalm wanted to live with God, watch and observe Him, and seek after Him. The psalmist knew that everything else he could have wished for paled in comparison to dwelling with God. When a person is in a relationship with Christ, desiring time with Him becomes the priority in life.

Imagine spending a whole day with Jesus. What would that day be like?

_____

_____

_____

_____

_____

_____

_____

_____

_____

_____

_____

_____

_____

_____

Know His Voice

The voice of the Lord is above the waters. The God of glory thunders—the Lord, above vast waters, the voice of the Lord in power, the voice of the Lord in splendor.

—PSALM 29:3–4

Christ refers to Himself as a shepherd in the New Testament. He says in John 10:27, "My sheep hear My voice, I know them, and they follow Me." Sheep know the voice of their shepherd, and they follow that voice. Being a Christian means learning the voice of your Shepherd and following what He says. God's voice is powerful. It is a strong force like thunder, and not because He yells, but because what He says is magnificent and worthy of being heard.

Train your ear to the splendor of God's voice. He has so much He wants to tell you.

Write out a prayer below and ask to be a better listener for God's voice.

_____

_____

_____

_____

_____

_____

_____

_____

_____

_____

_____

_____

_____

_____

Take Comfort

A man's steps are established by the Lord,
and He takes pleasure in his way. Though he falls,
he will not be overwhelmed, because the Lord holds his hand.

—PSALM 37:23–24

Christians mess up as much as non-Christians, but the difference is that God takes pleasure in the path of the Christian. Christians will stumble and fall, but the fall will not overwhelm them. They recover from the falls in life because God holds their hands, even as they are falling.

There is great comfort in knowing that God founded your path. There is even greater comfort in knowing that He walks with you regardless of the decisions you make on that path.

When was the last time you stumbled and
needed God to help you up?

_____

_____

_____

_____

_____

_____

_____

_____

_____

_____

_____

_____

_____

_____

Sealed

When you heard the message of truth, the gospel of your salvation, and when you believed in Him, you were also sealed with the promised Holy Spirit. He is the down payment of our inheritance, for the redemption of the possession, to the praise of His glory.

—EPHESIANS 1:13–14

Writing letters seem to be an art of the past. Taking the time to formulate what you want to say to someone, put it in writing, and then mail your words to them is something I wish we practiced more.

The recipient of a letter opens an envelope in order to retrieve the contents within. The letter remains secure in its envelope until the recipient breaks the seal. Someone who accepts Christ is like a sealed letter. A Christian is securely sealed by the Holy Spirit in the envelope of a relationship with Christ waiting to be delivered to the address of her heavenly inheritance.

Write a letter to God below about who you want to be and what you want to accomplish.

_____

_____

_____

_____

_____

_____

_____

_____

_____

_____

_____

_____

_____

_____

Christ's Body

And He put everything under His feet and appointed Him as head over everything for the church, which is His body, the fullness of the One who fills all things in every way.

—EPHESIANS 1:22–23

Christ is the head of the church, which means he has authority over the church. In fact, God gave Christ authority over everything for the sake of the church. The church is referred to as Christ's body. Being a Christian means being a part of this body of believers. Believers in the church show the fullness of Christ when they function out of their gifts. When each member of the church functions as God designed them to, the church is then fully reflecting Christ, which is exactly how God wants the church to function in this world. The church is to be the hands and feet of Christ, showing the world the love of Christ until He returns. Churches are not perfect places because they are made up of sinners, but we can trust that Christ, the head of the church, has the best interest of the church always in mind.

What talents can you use to help at your church?

_____

_____

_____

_____

_____

_____

_____

_____

_____

_____

_____

_____

_____

_____

_____

_____

Saved by Grace

But God, who is rich in mercy, because of His great love that He had for us, made us alive with the Messiah even though we were dead in trespasses. You are saved by grace!

—EPHESIANS 2:4–5

The gospel of Jesus Christ is that He did everything. We contribute nothing to the gift of salvation. We like to think that being good and doing good will save us, but our state of being before accepting Christ is like that of a dead person. We are like the stone statues in the White Witch's castle in Narnia. We have no breath or life in us until Christ breathes His breath of life into us. What saves us from our state of death is Christ. The gospel is Christ alone, not Christ's death plus our best efforts of being good. Only by His grace are we saved.

Write out your definition of grace.

Obey

Children, obey your parents as you would the Lord,
because this is right. Honor your father and mother, which is
the first commandment with a promise, so that it may go well
with you and that you may have a long life in the land.

—EPHESIANS 6:1–3

The Ten Commandments are divided into two categories—
our relationship with God and our relationship with
others. The first commandment of the second category
is to honor our mothers and fathers. Isn't it interesting
that the first commandment having to do with how we
relate with others is about our moms and dads? There is
a reason for this. How we relate to our moms and dads
determines how we interact with other people. As girls,
if we do not have good relationships with our dads, we
are prone to build unhealthy relationships with other
males. If we are disrespectful to our mothers, disrespect
will most likely find its way into our other relationships.
Learning to treat our parents with decency leads to a
long life of lasting friendships with others.

Share a favorite memory of a time spent with your parents.

_____

_____

_____

_____

_____

_____

_____

_____

_____

_____

_____

_____

_____

_____

_____

To Lose Is to Win

But everything that was a gain to me, I have considered to be a loss because of Christ. More than that, I also consider everything to be a loss in view of the surpassing value of knowing Christ Jesus my Lord. Because of Him I have suffered the loss of all things and consider them filth, so that I may gain Christ

—PHILIPPIANS 3:7–8

Most sports fans can relate to the taste of victory. Paul is saying in Philippians 3 to take all the wins you can imagine, take all the popularity you can imagine, and take all the fortune you can imagine, and none of it compares to knowing Christ. In fact he says that he will lose it all in order to get closer to Christ. He will trade all the wins and status for a relationship with Christ. You may be thinking that is a crazy trade, but Paul, like any other Christian, knows that a relationship with Christ is the only thing that will last. Christ is eternal. Everything else will eventually fade away. Winning streaks end, records get broken, somebody more popular comes along, and money can go as easily as it came, but a relationship with Christ is forever.

Compare your enthusiasm for Christ to your enthusiasm for your favorite sports team.

_____

_____

_____

_____

_____

_____

_____

_____

_____

_____

_____

_____

_____

_____

Belief in Heaven

But our citizenship is in heaven, from which we also eagerly wait for a Savior, the Lord Jesus Christ.

—PHILIPPIANS 3:20

Christians know that their current mailing address is not where they will permanently reside. They know that ultimately their home is in heaven. When Christ returns to this earth, He will usher believers into their new residence with Him. All will be made perfect. Creation and mankind will be perfect. Christians are eager for Christ's return so that they can live in the presence of God and experience perfection forever. There will be no colds, no stomach bugs, no need for glasses, no need for casts because there will be no broken bones, no acne, no need for braces, no arguments, no loss, and no pain.

What earthly problems are you most excited to ban from heaven?

Dwell on Truth

Finally brothers, whatever is true, whatever is honorable, whatever is just, whatever is pure, whatever is lovely, whatever is commendable—if there is any moral excellence and if there is any praise—dwell on these things.

—PHILIPPIANS 4:8

What we eat affects the productivity of our bodies. Who we spend time with affects our behavior. What we listen to affects our speech, and what we watch affects our thoughts. Christians need to monitor what they watch just as they need to monitor whom they hang out with. Christians are to think about what is moral, decent, and praiseworthy. Anything they watch that promotes impure thoughts should be eliminated from their repertoire. It is a small price to pay for the gift of life they are given through Christ.

Is there a friend, show, author, or band that should have much less time in your life?

_____

_____

_____

_____

_____

_____

_____

_____

_____

_____

_____

_____

_____

_____

A Clean Heart

**God, create a clean heart for me and renew
a steadfast spirit within me.**

—PSALM 51:10

We all have different versions of what "clean" is when it comes to cleaning. My mom's standard of cleanliness is incredible. I grew up in a house where the windows always sparkled, not only the floors but also the baseboards were immaculate, and bed sheets were line dried in the fresh air and then ironed. I appreciate how my mom kept our home. It makes me think of how God wants our hearts to be. He wants every corner in every room in our hearts to be unsoiled because He resides there when a person accepts Him as Lord and Savior. Our spirit is to be dedicated to the One who lives within us.

What rooms of your heart does God need to clean out?

_____

_____

_____

_____

_____

_____

_____

_____

_____

_____

_____

_____

_____

_____

A Broken Heart

The sacrifice pleasing to God is a broken spirit.
God, You will not despise a broken and humbled heart.

—PSALM 51:17

Animal blood sacrifices were made to God in Old Testament times to atone for sin. Christ made the final sacrifice for sin when He shed His blood on the cross. Christ's sacrifice satisfies atonement for any past, present, or future sin. In Psalm 51, King David is singing about a sacrifice we can make to God, not to atone for sin, but to draw us closer to Him. God is pleased with brokenness and humility in His children. It is much easier to teach a humbled person who sees her imperfections than a person who takes pride in her behavior and in how much she knows.

Does our world seem to value humility? What about you?

_____

_____

_____

_____

_____

_____

_____

_____

_____

_____

_____

_____

_____

_____

48

Hand Over Your Burdens

**Cast your burden on the Lord, and He will sustain you;
He will never allow the righteous to be shaken.**

—PSALM 55:22

We all have things that burden us. As females, our burdens usually fall in the camp of relationships. Most of our problems stem from a relationship. Most of our worry can be traced back to a relationship. Someone hurt our feelings, turned on us, or is not acting like herself.

Notice that this verse does not say you will be burden free. It simply says what to do with your burdens. You are to cast them on the Lord, not on Twitter or on another friend. When you turn to other sources with your burdens, it only complicates the burdens by inviting more people into the knowledge of what bothers you. God says to bring your burdens to Him. He will not spread what you share with Him, He will support you, and He will calm you.

Write out five worries below. Pray about them, and then draw a line through them.

_____

_____

_____

_____

_____

_____

_____

_____

_____

_____

_____

_____

_____

_____

_____

Every Knee Will Bow

By Myself I have sworn; Truth has gone from My mouth,
a word that will not be revoked: Every knee will
bow to Me, every tongue will swear allegiance.

—ISAIAH 45:23

Isaiah was a prophet. A prophet is someone God spoke
(or revealed Himself) through. Here, Isaiah is foretelling
how every single person will admit that Christ is Lord
at His return. Christians, as well as non-Christians,
will acknowledge in action and word that Jesus is Lord.
Right now, we do not see a lot of devotion to Jesus in
our world. One day that will change. People who deny
Christ now will confess that He is Lord at His return,
but these people will suffer eternal punishment because
they never chose to believe in Him before His return.
Christians, however, will experience eternity in the
presence of the Lord clothed in Christ's righteousness
because they declared Jesus as Lord while awaiting His
return.

Write a prayer below telling Jesus why you do or do not acknowledge Him as Lord?

_____

_____

_____

_____

_____

_____

_____

_____

_____

_____

_____

_____

_____

_____

_____

_____

At Rest in God

I am at rest in God alone; my salvation comes from Him.

—PSALM 62:1

A Christian knows that she needs saving. She knows that no trend will satisfy her deepest longings, no addiction will help her escape, and no amount of her own effort will save her. She knows that the only thing that will rescue her from her sin state is to accept Christ's righteousness. From God alone comes her salvation. She waits on God, not on fashion's latest fad or the newest version of technology. She knows that His saving grace saves her and gives her worth, not anything this world has to offer.

"I need to be saved from _____."

Thirst for God

**God, You are my God; I eagerly seek You.
I thirst for You; my body faints for You in a land
that is dry, desolate, and without water.**

—PSALM 63:1

At your age, school can be a "dry and weary land." If not school then maybe your family or a particular friendship has you weary. In the dry and weary land of life, you can either respond with doubt, by being angry or by retreating, or you can respond with trust. When you trust God, you seek Him to sustain you in the dry and weary land. You trust that God, not revenge or retaliation, will quench your thirst. You turn to God in the hard times.

Is there a relationship with a friend or family member that has you in a dry and weary land?

_____

_____

_____

_____

_____

_____

_____

_____

_____

_____

_____

_____

_____

52

The God of Creation

You establish the mountains by Your power,
robed with strength. You silence the roar of the seas,
the roar of their waves, and the tumult of the nations.

—PSALM 65:6–7

Being a Christian means that you know you worship the God who created the heavens and the earth. You worship the God who established the mountains and the seas. He gives height to the mountains by His strength, and He gives the waters their boundaries. These creations are not timid. They are fierce like God. Have you ever hiked or skied on a mountain or body surfed the waves of an ocean? You can only hike so high without the elevation effecting your breath and lungs. You can only ski certain grades of a mountain or else you would risk your life. When you ride a wave, you feel your body being tossed by its force. When you are in the mountains or the ocean, you are not on a kiddie playground. You are in the wild in the mountains, and you are in an aquatic adventure in the ocean. These creations display the splendor of the Almighty God of the Christian.

Which part of nature makes you marvel at God the most?

_____

_____

_____

_____

_____

_____

_____

_____

_____

_____

_____

_____

_____

_____

_____

Listen

"But My people did not listen to Me; Israel did not obey Me. So I gave them over to their stubborn hearts to follow their own plans. If only My people would listen to Me and Israel would follow My ways."

—PSALM 81:11–13

Jacob, one of our patriarchs, had his named changed to Israel when he wrestled with God (Genesis 32). The name Israel means "struggles with God." The Israelites were named after Jacob's new name, and we know from Old Testament stories that they were, in fact, a nation who struggled with God. In Psalm 81, we hear God say that the Israelites did not listen to Him so He gave them over to themselves. There is a plea in the psalm to listen to God's voice and walk in His ways. God makes the same plea to Christians, and He has recorded His voice for us in His Word. To hear Him, we must read His Word.

If God gave you a new name today, what would it be?

_____

_____

_____

_____

_____

_____

_____

_____

_____

_____

_____

_____

_____

One Mediator

For there is one God and one mediator between God and humanity, Christ Jesus, Himself human, who gave Himself—a ransom for all, a testimony at the proper time.

—1 TIMOTHY 2:5–6

Christians believe that there is one mediator between God and man, and that person is Christ. We believe there is a need for a mediator between God and ourselves because God is holy and we are not. Our sin causes a vast, indefinite gap between God and ourselves. Christ's death is what bridges the gap, and belief in His death is what makes the gap cease to exist. When God looks at a Christian, He sees Christ's righteousness instead of sin.

What does sin look like? What does righteousness look like?

_____

_____

_____

_____

_____

_____

_____

_____

_____

_____

_____

_____

_____

_____

Search

But from there, you will search for the LORD your God, and you will find Him when you seek Him with all your heart and all your soul.

—DEUTERONOMY 4:29

I wear contacts because my vision is horrible. My optometrist put me in gas permeable contact lens when I was in eighth grade. With gas permeable contacts, you wear the same contacts day after day. You take them out every night before bed, clean them really well, and soak them overnight. You do not get back-up lenses with gas permeable contacts. In fact, when I have dropped a contact down the sink drain, I immediately turn off the running water and unhook the P-trap under the sink. I rinse the P-trap out and pour its contents in a clear bowl to search for my little, blue-tinted contact. I go to all this trouble because replacing a gas permeable contact is expensive, getting in to see the optometrist takes time, and waiting on a new contact is a hassle. I also go to all the trouble of finding my contact because without one of my contacts, I cannot see!

When I search for the Lord with all of my heart, like I search for a lost contact, I find Him, and I can see!

What do you think it looks like to search for God?

_____

_____

_____

_____

_____

_____

_____

_____

_____

_____

_____

_____

_____

_____

56

Tree of Life

Long life is in her right hand; in her left, riches and honor. Her ways are pleasant, and all her paths, peaceful. She is a tree of life to those who embrace her, and those who hold on to her are happy.

—PROVERBS 3:16–18

Look at what these verses promise to the person who seeks wisdom. The list includes long life, riches, honor, pleasantness, and peace. This means that a wise person will have a full, meaningful life. Christians are to seek wisdom out of the understanding that nothing else in this life is as satisfying. Look also how these verses describe a wise person. A wise person is pleasant, peaceful, and blessed. The reason is given in verse 18. Wisdom is a tree of life to those who take hold of her. Remember how God placed the tree of life in the Garden of Eden with Adam and Eve, and how they ignored that tree and chose the tree of the knowledge of good and evil. Sin first entered the world because Adam and Eve chose the opposite of wisdom when they chose the other tree. Proverbs 3 reminds us that peace and blessings flow from choosing wisdom, the tree of life.

Could wisdom bring life to one of your current situations? How?

_____

_____

_____

_____

_____

_____

_____

_____

_____

_____

_____

_____

_____

_____

_____

_____

Wisdom

The Lord founded the earth by wisdom and established the heavens by understanding. By His knowledge the watery depths broke open, and the clouds dripped with dew.

—PROVERBS 3:19–20

Starting a business takes time and preparation. A person does not haphazardly create a business. A lot of research and planning goes into starting a business before the doors of that business even open.

Christians believe that God started the business of the world. He created everything that we see. He started it all and brought it all into existence. We are told from Scripture that wisdom was with God when He created the world. Proverbs 8:22–31 gives a further description of wisdom existing with God when He created the world. The wisdom that a Christian is called to seek is the counsel of God Himself, who so wisely created all things. That is quite a powerful source of understanding that we get to tap into if we choose.

In what ways do you hope to be wiser two years from now? What about ten years from now?

_____

_____

_____

_____

_____

_____

_____

_____

_____

_____

_____

_____

_____

Follow Instructions

Hold on to instruction; don't let go.
Guard it, for it is your life.

—PROVERBS 4:13

If you cook or bake, you know that it is important to follow the recipe. If you have traveled, you know that it is critical to follow directions. A delectable dessert or arriving at your destination is the result of following instructions. Christians are also given a set of instructions to follow in the Word of God. God laid out His directions for loving Him and loving others in Scripture. When we guard what He says by following His instruction, we gain wisdom and life.

Write out a recipe for following God.

_____

_____

_____

_____

_____

_____

_____

_____

_____

_____

_____

_____

_____

Life and Health

My son, pay attention to my words; listen closely to my sayings. Don't lose sight of them; keep them within your heart. For they are life to those who find them, and health to one's whole body.

—PROVERBS 4:20–22

Solomon, the son of King David, wrote the book of Proverbs. The words of wisdom that Solomon wrote to his children were instructions his father taught him (Proverbs 4:3–4). Parents know that they know best and that their children's lives will be richer if they choose to follow their parents' instructions. These verses are applicable to our relationship with our heavenly parent. When we keep God's instructions in our hearts, we find health, life, and healing. We need these three promises in a world filled with emotional disease, spiritual death, and sickness of the heart.

When the world says one thing and God says another, how does God's instruction protect you?

Your Words

**Don't let your mouth speak dishonestly,
and don't let your lips talk deviously.**

—PROVERBS 4:24

There is a lot of crooked speech and devious talk that occurs in the girls' bathroom, the lunchroom, and the hallways at school. There is also a lot of crooked speech that happens through typed or texted words. As a Christian, you are called to put away any devious talk whether you are communicating through written or spoken word. Check your speech and the motives behind what you say, text, or post. This is a daily check needed several times a day.

What kind of words have you spoken, typed, and texted today?

_____

_____

_____

_____

_____

_____

_____

_____

_____

_____

_____

_____

_____

_____

_____

Look Straight Ahead

Let your eyes look forward; fix your gaze straight ahead.
Carefully consider the path for your feet,
and all your ways will be established. Don't turn
to the right or to the left; keep your feet away from evil.

—PROVERBS 4:25–27

What catches your eye? Is it a particular magazine, article of clothing, or certain guy? Girls' eyes are drawn to shoes, purses, fashion, and anything that is "in." Our attention can also be drawn to the business of others. God calls us to more than that, though. God says to consider our own paths and not the paths of others who are to our right or left. We are to reflect on ourselves and not others.

How much time do you spend considering other girls, what they are doing and wearing, and whom they are hanging out with? God says to ponder your own path. When your thoughts swerve off of your path and onto someone else's, get them back in your lane. Your footsteps are more secure when you fix your gaze straight ahead rather than on how you measure up to others.

Has someone or something been filling your thoughts lately?

_____

_____

_____

_____

_____

_____

_____

_____

_____

_____

_____

_____

_____

_____

Train for Godliness

**In fact, we labor and strive for [godliness],
because we have put our hope in the living God, who is
the Savior of everyone, especially of those who believe.**

—1 TIMOTHY 4:10

In Paul's first letter to Timothy, he tells Timothy to train for godliness. If you have ever trained for a race or competition, you know that it takes a lot of work. There is no difference in training for godliness. It takes a lot of work, and you have to put time into the training. If you are training to be an elite gymnast, you cannot send your mom or a friend to practice the uneven bars or vault for you. In the same way, you have to labor for godliness yourself. You cannot leave your godliness up to your mom, dad, friend, or youth pastor.

Just as you train for a race or competition in hopes of a medal, you train for godliness because you hope in the person of Christ. He is not only your hope; He is the One who gets you through the strenuous workouts of godliness.

What are some ways to "train" for godliness?

_____

_____

_____

_____

_____

_____

_____

_____

_____

_____

_____

_____

_____

_____

Be an Example

**Let no one despise your youth; instead,
you should be an example to the believers
in speech, in conduct, in love, in faith, in purity.**

—1 TIMOTHY 4:12

You are never too young to be an example of godliness. You have daily opportunities to share the gospel through your speech and through your actions. Sometimes how you conduct yourself will say more about what you believe than if you used actual words. An Italian saint named Francis of Assisi said, "Preach the gospel, and when necessary, use words."

You can preach the gospel through simple acts of love, by remaining faithful to your beliefs no matter what the circumstance, and through making good decisions about remaining pure. Your conduct is just as powerful an evangelistic tool as your words.

Try to count the number of people who saw you today. What kind of girl did all those people see?

_____

_____

_____

_____

_____

_____

_____

_____

_____

_____

_____

_____

_____

_____

_____

_____

64

You Are Free

**The Spirit of the Lord God is on Me,
because the Lord has anointed Me to bring good news
to the poor. He has sent Me to heal the brokenhearted, to pro-
claim liberty to the captives and freedom to the prisoners.**

—ISAIAH 61:1

Have you ever played capture the flag and been captured by the other team as you attempted to get their flag? If you have, then you know how good it feels to get back in the game when a member of your team tags you out of jail and sets you free. There are times in life when sin captures you and holds you in its jail. Christ quotes Isaiah 61 in Luke 4 and says that He is the One who mends broken hearts and frees people from the prison of sin. Being a Christian means Christ tagged your heart and freed you from the captivity of sin. Christ's blood freed you from being a slave to sin.

When was the last time you were brokenhearted?

You Are in a Fight

Fight the good fight for the faith; take hold of eternal life that you were called to and have made a good confession about in the presence of many witnesses.

—1 TIMOTHY 6:12

When a person accepts Christ, she enters a fight. In the ring with her is her opponent, Satan. The outcome of the fight is already determined. It is a win for her and loss for him. But before she can experience the victory, she will need to dodge some hits and throw some punches. Satan knows the timer will soon sound ending the fight, so he tries to knock down his opponent as many times as he can. When he throws his jabs and uppercuts, she fights back and remains standing. What keeps her vertical during the fight is that her eyes are fixed on the One who conquered her enemy for her and the promise of being with him forever when the fight is over.

What does it take to be a good fighter against Satan?

_____

_____

_____

_____

_____

_____

_____

_____

_____

_____

_____

_____

_____

_____

The Perfect Coach

All Scripture is inspired by God and is profitable for teaching, for rebuking, for correcting, for training in righteousness.

—2 TIMOTHY 3:16

If you play a sport, you have a coach who continually teaches you about that sport, expresses sharp disapproval when you mess up, corrects your technique, and trains you through conditioning your body for the big game. When it comes to being a Christian and living a godly life, the Bible is your coach. In God's Word you will find beneficial teaching, stern disapproval of some of your heart's motives, a standard for your thoughts, and guidelines for godliness. You can trust all the instructions given to you in God's Word because He is the One who wrote it.

List some ways that being a Christian is like being an athlete.

_____

_____

_____

_____

_____

_____

_____

_____

_____

_____

_____

_____

_____

_____

_____

Mercy

But when the kindness of God our Savior and His love for mankind appeared, He saved us—not by works of righteousness that we had done, but according to His mercy, through the washing of regeneration and renewal by the Holy Spirit.

—TITUS 3:4–5

If a police officer pulled me over for speeding and did not give me a ticket for my offense, he would be showing me mercy. Getting a speeding ticket that I deserved would be justice, but not getting a ticket would be merciful of the police officer. In a similar way, God holding back from me the death that I deserve because of sin is merciful of Him. Instead of God issuing me the ticket of death, He issues the ticket to His Son. Christ pays for my offense.

Is there someone in your life who needs your mercy?

_____

_____

_____

_____

_____

_____

_____

_____

_____

_____

_____

_____

_____

_____

_____

God's Network

**Long ago God spoke to the fathers by the prophets
at different times and in different ways. In these last days,
He has spoken to us by His Son. God has appointed Him
heir of all things and made the universe through Him.**

—HEBREWS 1:1–2

When I was young, I talked to my friends on a phone that was plugged into a wall in my house. I could only get hold of my friends when neither of our telephone lines was busy. Once both of our phone lines were open, we could finally talk. Now that I am older, I continue to communicate with my friends, but the means by which I talk to them has changed. Today, when I talk to my friends, there is no cord to my phone that confines me to one place. I can talk or text with my friends from inside or outside of my home.

In Old Testament times, God spoke to His friends through prophets. Prophets stayed plugged into God. They proclaimed His thoughts to His friends. Now, God speaks to His friends through His Son. Since Christ's death and resurrection, Christ is God's network for speaking to the world, and this network has a lot of coverage!

How is prayer a good means of communication?

_____

_____

_____

_____

_____

_____

_____

_____

_____

_____

_____

_____

_____

_____

Christ Suffered

But we do see Jesus—made lower than the angels for a short time so that by God's grace He might taste death for everyone—crowned with glory and honor because of His suffering in death.

—HEBREWS 2:9

You may have experienced the death of someone you love. If you have, you know death is sad, and sometimes people suffer prior to their death. Christ's suffering in death is different than mankind's suffering. Christ's death was agonizing because He was the sacrifice for all sin—past, present, and future. What Christ felt in death was God's righteous judgment (or wrath). As Christ sacrificially endured the unbearable weight of sin, God turned His back on Him. God, who is holy, could not look at the sin on Christ. Christians will never experience the agony of separation from God, even in their own deaths, because Christ experienced it for them.

How is death easier for Christians?

_____

_____

_____

_____

_____

_____

_____

_____

_____

_____

_____

_____

_____

_____

_____

The Sword of the Word

For the word of God is living and effective and sharper than any double-edged sword, penetrating as far as the separation of soul and spirit, joints and marrow. It is able to judge the ideas and thoughts of the heart.

—HEBREWS 4:12

A sword is a weapon that pierces the body. A sword wound could be as deep as the sword is long. The writer of Hebrews speaks of God's Word as a sword, but this sword is a weapon that pierces us for our benefit not our harm. God's Word pierces us to heal us not to wound us. As God's Word penetrates our hearts and minds, we are changed. We take on a different attitude and stature from reading the Bible. God's Word is one knife we do want to "go under."

List five ways you can spend more time with God's Word this week.

_____

_____

_____

_____

_____

_____

_____

_____

_____

_____

_____

_____

_____

_____

Our High Priest

For we do not have a high priest who is unable
to sympathize with our weaknesses, but One who has
been tested in every way as we are, yet without sin.

—HEBREWS 4:15

Your school most likely has a student government made up of representatives from each grade. Your grade probably selected and voted on one or more students to represent your grade as a whole. These representatives serve on behalf of your grade by keeping the best interests of your grade in mind.

In Old Testament times, the people who represented the Israelites in matters related to God were called high priests (5:1). These men were not appointed by the people, but selected by God for the people. In the New Testament, we learn that God selected Christ to serve as our representative, or high priest. What sets Christ apart from any other high priest or representative is that He serves in His role without sin. Although He is perfect, He still relates to us as He serves us.

How is Jesus a better high priest than those of the Old Testament?

One Sacrifice

He doesn't need to offer sacrifices every day, as high priests do—first for their own sins, then for those of the people. He did this once for all when He offered Himself.

—HEBREWS 7:27

High priests offered a lot of sacrifices to God on behalf of the Israelites. The sacrifices were made in the tabernacle, a structure that God had the Israelites build so that He could dwell among them. In New Testament times, God came to dwell among His people in the flesh through the person of Christ with a mission to offer His life as the final sacrifice to atone for all sin. He offered His life in death so that we might have life now and after death.

Why do you think Christ's death on the cross was the final sacrifice that God required for sin?

_____

_____

_____

_____

_____

_____

_____

_____

_____

_____

_____

_____

_____

_____

_____

Most Holy Place

**He entered the most holy place once for all,
not by the blood of goats and calves,
but by His own blood, having obtained eternal redemption.**

—HEBREWS 9:12

There were three parts to the tabernacle where sacrifices were made—the courtyard, the holy place, and the most holy place. The most holy place housed the ark of the covenant, which held the Ten Commandments, and only the high priest had access to the most holy place. The most holy place sat behind a curtain, and the high priest entered it once a year on the Day of Atonement when he would make amends for all the sins of all the Israelites for the entire year.

The high priest had access once a year to the place that held God's law. He obtained this access through the blood of animals. Today, anyone who believes in Christ has access to God's words anytime through the blood of Christ.

How has God shown us that He wants a personal relationship with us?

_____

_____

_____

_____

_____

_____

_____

_____

_____

_____

_____

_____

_____

_____

_____

_____

74

Christ Is Coming Again

And just as it is appointed for people to die once—and after this, judgment—so also the Messiah, having been offered once to bear the sins of many, will appear a second time, not to bear sin, but to bring salvation to those who are waiting for Him.

—HEBREWS 9:27–28

Christ first came to earth as a baby. The fact that the Son of God came to earth by taking on human flesh is amazing. What is even more remarkable is that He chose to come into the world as a helpless infant dependent on others to feed Him, carry Him, and wipe Him. Christ went through the stages of development just like we do, although, He did it perfectly because He is God. Christ could have chosen to come into the world as a man (or at least after puberty!), but instead, He chose the humblest of all stages. Then, as a grown man, He gave his life.

Christ brought the sacrifice of His life in His first coming, but the next time He appears, He will bring the eternal life He has promised to those who believe in Him.

Why do you think Jesus came to earth as a poor child instead of a powerful king?

_____

_____

_____

_____

_____

_____

_____

_____

_____

_____

_____

_____

_____

_____

Do Not Waver

Let us hold on to the confession of our hope without wavering, for He who promised is faithful.

—HEBREWS 10:23

I am incapable of making simple decisions for myself. At a restaurant, I will vacillate over all the menu options. If I am trying to purchase a garment, I will waver between all the assortments of clothing options. I even hesitate over which bundle of bananas to buy at the grocery store. I attribute my indecisiveness to becoming a mom. I use all my energy being decisive in regards to my children, and so I have become indecisive when it comes to insignificant matters in my own life.

God tells us never to waver when it comes to our faith. We should never fluctuate when it comes to what we confess about Christ. We can securely stand on the sacrifice that Christ made for us.

What about Christ's sacrifice assures you that faith in Christ is real?

_____

_____

_____

_____

_____

_____

_____

_____

_____

_____

_____

_____

_____

_____

_____

Faith

**Now faith is the reality of what is hoped for,
the proof of what is not seen.**

—HEBREWS 11:1

Faith in Christ means you are sure that Christ has come, Christ died and was resurrected, and Christ is coming again. Your faith gives you the guarantee that Christ will return to make all things anew. God's Word is your proof of what you believe. Even though you did not live at the time He lived, you know from Scripture that God came down and took on human flesh, died a death that you deserved, and conquered death with His resurrection. Even though Christ has not yet returned, you know from God's Word that He is coming back to establish His kingdom fully. Just like Noah believed God when He told him to prepare for a flood that was coming, you believe God's Word as it teaches you to prepare for Christ's return.

Do you feel that you need to prepare for Christ's return?

_____

_____

_____

_____

_____

_____

_____

_____

_____

_____

_____

_____

_____

_____

_____

The Ultimate Artist

By faith we understand that the universe was created by God's command, so that what is seen has been made from things that are not visible.

—HEBREWS 11:3

When I admire a beautiful piece of artwork, I do not think that it just appeared. I know that the art is the result of a skilled artist. I may never be in the presence of the artist whose masterpiece I admire, but I know that the artist exists.

The universe is God's artwork. We see the world around us, but cannot see the Artist who made the world. We see glimpses of Him in His Word and through the person of Christ, and our faith helps us know that one day we will forever be in His presence.

Write down five nouns that describe God. Was "Artist" one of them?

_____

_____

_____

_____

_____

_____

_____

_____

_____

_____

_____

_____

_____

_____

_____

Keep Your Eyes on Jesus

Let us run with endurance the race that lies before us, keeping our eyes on Jesus, the source and perfecter of our faith, who for the joy that lay before Him endured a cross and despised the shame and has sat down at the right hand of God's throne.

—HEBREWS 12:1–2

Look back at all that is said about Jesus in these two verses. He is the source of our faith, meaning He is the foundation to all that we believe. He is the one who perfects our faith, meaning He refines us, as we believe in what He accomplished. He endured the cross because He took joy in knowing that the sacrifice of His life would save us. He also sat down at the right hand of God, which means that He has accomplished all that He needed to and now rules in authority with God the Father.

This King is the One to whom our eyes should be glued. We should look constantly to Him as we run the race of life before us.

What are the benefits of keeping our eyes on Jesus?

_____

_____

_____

_____

_____

_____

_____

_____

_____

_____

_____

_____

_____

_____

A City

If they were thinking about where they came from, they would have had an opportunity to return. But they now desire a better place—a heavenly one. Therefore God is not ashamed to be called their God, for He has prepared a city for them.

—HEBREWS 11:15–16

Hebrews 11 lists people of faith from the Old Testament. Verses 15 and 16 reference those people, saying that it was because of their faith in God that they thought about the land he had promised them, the land of Canaan, rather than the land they came from. For the entire time that they were a part of the journey to the Promised Land, they did not consider the things they left behind. Christians also should think about the promise of what is ahead for them rather than what they have given up to follow Christ. We should consider the ultimate Promised Land. What God has promised all believers is more than a place in the clouds where we will float around and play harps. He has promised a land, a kingdom, and a city we will never tire of exploring as we run and play there in our resurrected bodies.

What do you think will be the best part about heaven?

_____

_____

_____

_____

_____

_____

_____

_____

_____

_____

_____

_____

_____

_____

_____

Seek the Kingdom

**For we do not have an enduring city here;
instead, we seek the one to come.**

—HEBREWS 13:14

Christians know that they are in temporary housing until Christ returns. Their permanent housing is the "city" that God promises in His Word. God tells believers to seek that promised home of the future. Christians are to cast their eyes on the promise of what is ahead rather than what is right before them. They are to make decisions and live life in light of a coming Kingdom.

This kind of forward thinking changes how a person lives. She suddenly becomes least concerned with the things of this world as she focuses her attention on the promised kingdom of God.

How does focusing on the coming Kingdom change your priorities?

_____

_____

_____

_____

_____

_____

_____

_____

_____

_____

_____

_____

_____

_____

With Christ

"I am going away to prepare a place for you.
If I go away and prepare a place for you,
I will come back and receive you to Myself,
so that where I am you may be also."

—JOHN 14:2–3

Imagine a dating relationship between a man and a woman where the man is a soldier who has been deployed for war. He loves the woman he is dating and wants to marry her, so he proposes before he leaves the country. She loves her man and graciously accepts his marriage proposal, reassuring him that she will wait a lifetime for his return. He goes away to fight in battle, leaving his fiancée behind, and then after finishing his duties, he comes back for his love.

You are God's love. He has fought His battle and gone away, but He is coming back for you so that you can be with Him forever. The only thing is, He is waiting on you to say yes to his proposal. If you have not already accepted Christ, then I pray that you will so you can have the promise of being with Christ forever.

How is a relationship with Christ better than human relationships?

The Importance of Articles

Jesus told him, "I am the way, the truth, and the life.
No one comes to the Father except through Me."

—JOHN 14:6

In your English class, you have learned or will learn about articles. *A, an,* and *the* are articles that modify nouns. *The* is a definite article, meaning it expresses the specificity of a noun. *A* and *an* are indefinite articles. They refer to nonspecific nouns.

Look back at John 14:6, and notice that Jesus uses the definite article *the*. He does not say that He is just a member of a group of ways to the Father. He says He is *the* way. He is not just one of many truths. He is *the* truth. Jesus is not a way of life. He is *the* life. He is the bridge across the great canyon of sin that brings us to the Father.

Why do you think God gave us only one way to reach Him?

83

Keep His Words

"If you love Me, you will keep My commands."

—JOHN 14:15

The Five Love Languages is a book by Gary Chapman that teaches spouses how to love one another. Rather than loving your spouse in a way that you would feel loved, the book challenges you to love your spouse in a way that makes him feel loved. The principle of the book can extend into any relationship. You can love someone by speaking encouraging words, spending quality time together, giving gifts, doing acts of service, or expressing physical touch. My love language is quality time. I feel most loved by a person when we spend time together. It does not matter what we are doing just as long as we get quality time together.

God tells us to love Him by keeping His words. He feels most loved when we do what He says. His words have our best interest in mind, so we show Him our love when we trust what He tells us in His Word. Obedience is God's love language.

How can you speak God's love language?

Remain in Christ

"Remain in Me, and I in you. Just as a branch is unable to produce fruit by itself unless it remains on the vine, so neither can you unless you remain in Me. I am the vine; you are the branches. The one who remains in Me and I in him produces much fruit, because you can do nothing without Me."

—JOHN 15:4–5

My Kitchen-Aid electric mixer cannot produce the batter it makes unless it is plugged into the outlet. My mixer's cord has to remain in the outlet in order to mix the batter that then produces delicious baked goods. You are like my electric mixer. You must remain plugged into God, who is like the outlet supplying you with energy to produce fruit. The fruit from your life should impact others like the batter from my mixer impacts those who enjoy the yummy desserts it yields. You must remain plugged into the outlet of God in order to produce His delicacies.

Describe how your life feels different when you
are plugged into God than when you are not.

_____

_____

_____

_____

_____

_____

_____

_____

_____

_____

_____

_____

_____

_____

_____

Joy

"If you keep My commands you will remain in My love, just as I have kept My Father's commands and remain in His love. I have spoken these things to you so that My joy may be in you and your joy may be complete."

—JOHN 15:10–11

Jesus shows us what obedience looks like by the way He lived His life. He was perfectly obedient to His Father. When Satan tempted Jesus in the wilderness, Jesus did not show His power and authority; He demonstrated His obedience. He remained in His Father's love by keeping His Father's commands.

Jesus does not give us an example of how to remain in God's love. There is not a three-step program to remaining in God's love in Scripture. Instead, Jesus says to be founded in His obedience and then we will experience true joy.

Think about a time when you did the right thing even though it was hard. Did you feel joyful afterward?

_____

_____

_____

_____

_____

_____

_____

_____

_____

_____

_____

_____

_____

_____

Friend

"I do not call you slaves anymore, because a slave doesn't know what his master is doing. I have called you friends, because I have made known to you everything I have heard from My Father."

—JOHN 15:15

I do not know of a religion, outside of Christianity, where the god of that religion died for his followers, resurrected from the dead, and refers to his followers as friends. God the Son did all three. Christ considers us worthy enough to be in His inner circle. He tells us things that will benefit our lives. He shares His rescue mission with us, performs that mission on the cross for us, and then leaves us with everything else He has heard from the Father in His Word. Who would not want a friend like Jesus!

What can we learn about friendship from Jesus?

_____

_____

_____

_____

_____

_____

_____

_____

_____

_____

_____

_____

_____

_____

The Spirit

"When the Counselor comes, the One I will send to you from the Father—the Spirit of truth who proceeds from the Father—He will testify about Me."

—JOHN 15:26

Christianity professes a triune God. God is three persons in one substance

In John 15, God the Son is saying farewell to His disciples. He tells them that though He is returning to the Father, He is leaving them with the Spirit. He tells them (and us) that the role of the Spirit is to declare the Son of God. The Spirit gives testimony about Christ. Even though we cannot talk to Christ in person, we know what He thinks about the things we discuss with Him because the Spirit reveals it to us through the truth of His Word.

What has the Spirit revealed to you recently through God's Word?

_____

_____

_____

_____

_____

_____

_____

_____

_____

_____

_____

_____

_____

_____

_____

88

From Suffering to Joy

"When a woman is in labor she has pain because her time has come. But when she has given birth to a child, she no longer remembers the suffering because of the joy that a person has been born into the world. So you also have sorrow now. But I will see you again. Your hearts will rejoice, and no one will rob you of your joy."

—JOHN 16:21–22

When a woman is having a baby, she goes into labor which is painful. Once the baby is delivered, the mom no longer considers the pain she was in. She is too overjoyed by the little life she holds in her arms.

Jesus' disciples were filled with pain at the thought of Him no longer being with them. Jesus tells them that their hearts will rejoice when they see Him again just as a mom forgets her pain when she finally holds her baby. The disciples do forget their sorrow when they see Christ at His resurrection because they are overjoyed to see Christ at His resurrection.

Christians also have the promise of seeing Christ at His Second Coming. We will forget our sorrows, suffering, and pain, and joy will overcome us as we stand in the presence of Christ.

What do you think the Second Coming will be like?

_____

_____

_____

_____

_____

_____

_____

_____

_____

_____

_____

_____

_____

_____

Ask

"In that day you will not ask Me anything. I assure you:
Anything you ask the Father in My name, He will give you.
Until now you have asked for nothing in My name.
Ask and you will receive, so that your joy may be complete."

—JOHN 16:23–24

My two boys ask a lot of my husband and me because they are young. They ask us to feed them, read to them, lie beside them at bedtime, take them to the bathroom, carry them, draw for them, and sing to them. One day, they will not ask us for these things because there will be no need. They will be grown men.

Right now, we need a lot from God, and as our Father, He is happy to give us what we ask when it is in our best interest. One day when Jesus returns, we will not ask anything of God because we will not need anything. We will live in perfection as perfect beings. We will have everything that we could possibly want or need. That day, however, has not come, so Christ tells us to pray to the Father in His name.

What things do you need today that you might not need five years from now?

_____

_____

_____

_____

_____

_____

_____

_____

_____

_____

_____

_____

_____

_____

The Word

In the beginning was the Word, and the Word was with God, and the Word was God.

—JOHN 1:1

When we read this verse in context, we know that the Word is Jesus. Read the verse again substituting "the Word" with Jesus' name. "In the beginning was Jesus." He was with God and was God before the creation of the world. The phrase "in the beginning" that John uses reminds us of Genesis 1:1 where we are told that "in the beginning, God created the heavens and the earth." John expands on Genesis 1:1 by letting us know that Jesus was with God and was God from the beginning.

Why is it hard for us to imagine that God has _always_ existed?

_____

_____

_____

_____

_____

_____

_____

_____

_____

_____

_____

_____

_____

_____

_____

_____

Light of Christ

Life was in Him, and that life was the light of men. That light shines in the darkness, yet the darkness did not overcome it.

—JOHN 1:4–5

The first thing God created was light (Genesis 1:3). He simply spoke and light came to be. God took the light He created and separated it from darkness. John 1 speaks about another light. This light was not created but has always existed with the Father. This light conquered darkness and shines in mankind. This light took on flesh, and His life becomes our light and our hope. All we have to do to receive the light of Christ is accept Him.

Light and darkness—which is more comforting? Which feels safer? Which feels happier?

_____

_____

_____

_____

_____

_____

_____

_____

_____

_____

_____

_____

_____

_____

Rejected

He was in the world, and the world was created through Him, yet the world did not recognize Him. He came to His own, and His own people did not receive Him.

—JOHN 1:10–11

Imagine one of your childhood friends, who climbed up the ranks socially at school with your help, turning on you after all you did for her. She decided one day to snub you at lunch by not letting you sit with her and your other friends. When you walked up to the table, she put something in the seat you normally sit in and said that the seat was saved for someone else. Confused and hurt, you turn to walk away and find another seat.

God came to the world He created through the person of Christ, and the world rejected Him. The world places lots of other things in the rightful seat of Christ. Instead of turning and walking away, He laid down His life.

Have you ever felt rejected? What did you do?

_____

_____

_____

_____

_____

_____

_____

_____

_____

_____

_____

_____

_____

_____

_____

Born of God

But to all who did receive Him, He gave them the right to be children of God, to those who believe in His name, who were born, not of blood, or of the will of the flesh, or of the will of man, but of God.

—JOHN 1:12–13

If you are a Christian, you are a child of God. You are still your mother and father's child, but you are first a child of God. God created you and brought you into this world through your mother, and He birthed you again when you received Him as Lord and Savior of your life. Remember that He bore your faith. You can take no credit in accepting Him. You believe in His name not because a blood relative does and not because you decided to on your own. You believe in Him because He pricked your heart and opened it to invite Him in.

If you are God's child, do you look like Him?

_____

_____

_____

_____

_____

_____

_____

_____

_____

_____

_____

_____

_____

_____

_____

The Word Took On Flesh

**The Word became flesh and took up residence among us.
We observed His glory, the glory as the One and
Only Son from the Father, full of grace and truth.**

—JOHN 1:14

The Word, who was with God and was God in the beginning, became man. He took on flesh and entered the world He created. He lived among us and many observed His glory. He was fully God and fully man. He was sovereign yet went through the physical and mental stages of development. He was perfect yet felt the torment of temptation. He was omnipresent yet walked the earth in one particular location. He was all knowing as an infant, loving as a hormonal pubescent teen, and a bridegroom to the world even though He was single. This God of ours is glorious. We must not try to fit Him in our little box of spirituality.

Is it helpful for you to know that Jesus was tempted too?

_____

_____

_____

_____

_____

_____

_____

_____

_____

_____

_____

_____

_____

_____

95

You Are Married

Adulteresses! Don't you know that friendship with the world is hostility toward God? So whoever wants to be the world's friend becomes God's enemy.

—JAMES 4:4

Adultery is being unfaithful to your spouse. You may think adultery does not apply to you because you are not married, but if you are a Christian, you do have a spouse. The New Testament speaks about how Christ is the believer's bridegroom. If you are a Christian, you are in a sense married to God. God is asking you to be a faithful partner to Him by not making friends with the world. Here are some ways you can honor His requests. Do not turn to the world to measure your worth; turn to the One who designed you. Do not look to the world for the answer of who you are, but look in the eyes of your Groom who made you and knows you. Do not ask the world to measure your beauty; ask Christ to show you how beautiful you are to Him. His blood responds to you and shouts from the mountaintops, "You are so worthy, spectacular, and beautiful that I died for you!"

Write a prayer below to thank God for all the ways He made you worthy and wonderful.

_____

_____

_____

_____

_____

_____

_____

_____

_____

_____

_____

_____

_____

_____

_____

96

Believe

**You love Him, though you have not seen Him.
And though not seeing Him now, you believe in Him
and rejoice with inexpressible and glorious joy.**

—1 PETER 1:8

Being a Christian means you believe in God, whom you cannot see. You can see results of His blessings and see His love in your life, but you cannot physically see Him. You can read in the Bible about a time when He was seen through the person of Christ, but you cannot see Christ yourself. This is where belief enters the Christian faith. As a Christian, you believe what *was* seen. You believe what is written about God walking with Adam in the garden, promising Abraham numerous descendants, wrestling with Jacob, talking to Moses in a burning bush, and crossing the Israelites through the Red Sea. You believe what is written about Christ coming to the world as a baby, teaching about His coming Kingdom, performing miracles, dying a death by crucifixion, rising from the dead, ascending into heaven, and returning one day. These are the unseen things a Christian believes.

Is there anything else you believe exists but you've never physically seen? What about wind?

_____

_____

_____

_____

_____

_____

_____

_____

_____

_____

_____

_____

_____

_____

_____

_____

Redeemed

For you know that you were redeemed from your empty way of life inherited from the fathers, not with perishable things like silver or gold, but with the precious blood of Christ, like that of a lamb without defect or blemish.

—1 PETER 1:18–19

You have willingly sold yourself into the slavery of sin. Since birth, sin has been your master. This is your inheritance from Adam. Then a second Adam, that is Christ, came to buy you back since you are rightfully His. The debt you accumulated while being in slavery, He paid off. He paid it off not with money, but with His precious blood. The debt required blood because only blood can atone for sin, so He poured out His blood for you. His blood frees you from your sin master only when you accept what He did for you.

How much do you value the freedom that Christ's life, death, and resurrection gives you?

_____

_____

_____

_____

_____

_____

_____

_____

_____

_____

_____

_____

_____

_____

_____

98

Aching to Be with God

How lovely is Your dwelling place, Lord of Hosts. I long and yearn for the courts of the Lord; my heart and flesh cry out for the living God.

—PSALM 84:1–2

As girls we long to feel significant. We love feeling special and made over. God longs for us to feel that way about Him. He wants us to long for Him, to yearn to be with Him. The more we turn to Him, the more we experience Him, and the more we experience Him, the more we yearn to be with Him. The more time we spend with God, the more we appreciate our time with Him. We begin to realize it is better to be in His courts than anywhere else.

Do you spend more time with God today than you did a year ago?

_____

_____

_____

_____

_____

_____

_____

_____

_____

_____

_____

_____

_____

_____

_____

_____

Hover

He will cover you with His feathers; you will take refuge under His wings. His faithfulness will be a protective shield.

—PSALM 91:4

Before the Israelites left Egypt, there was a really big event that happened called "the Passover." The Passover coincided with the tenth plague, which brought death to every firstborn. God protected His people from the plague by instituting the Passover. On the evening of the day of the tenth plague, the Israelites had specific instructions to follow to protect their household from death. One of those instructions was to spread the blood of a perfect lamb on their doorframes. When the angel of death came at midnight to strike down every firstborn, it saw the blood and passed over the Israelites homes. God hovered over the homes marked with blood to protect His people.

In Psalm 91:4, we get the same image of God hovering as a mother bird protecting her young. God shields with His feathers those who have spread the blood of the Perfect Lamb over their hearts.

Imagine yourself as a baby bird being protected under God's wing. How would that feel?

_____

_____

_____

_____

_____

_____

_____

_____

_____

_____

_____

_____

_____

_____

You Have Everything

His divine power has given us everything required for life and godliness through the knowledge of Him who called us by His own glory and goodness.

—2 PETER 1:3

My plan as a parent is to invest in my children so that they will have all the tools they need to lead a successful, godly life. My oldest is only twelve years away from being eighteen. I have twelve years to listen, support, encourage, and play with him. I have just twelve years left of vacationing with him and teaching him life lessons. Before I know it, he will be a grown man who has everything he needs to live on his own.

Similarly, Christians have everything they need from their Father. He has given His children all knowledge required for life and godliness. Fortunately, God's parenting plan is different than mine. God prepares His children for greater, not less, dependency on Him. As my children grow, they should become more independent. As Christians grow, they should become more dependent on their Father.

Whom do you depend on most in life?